Be a Cave Explorer!

Contents

Written by Catherine Baker

Collins

Fantastic caves

Lots of people visit caves each year – for good reasons.

Caves are astonishing! They are fun for families ... and sports people.

How caves were made

Some caves were formed by the sea.

Strong waves crashed on this beach, turning the rocks into caves.

Some caves were made when rain leaked into rock.

6

The rain made the rock weak, so caves formed.

Exploring caves

By exploring caves, experts can tell us their stories.

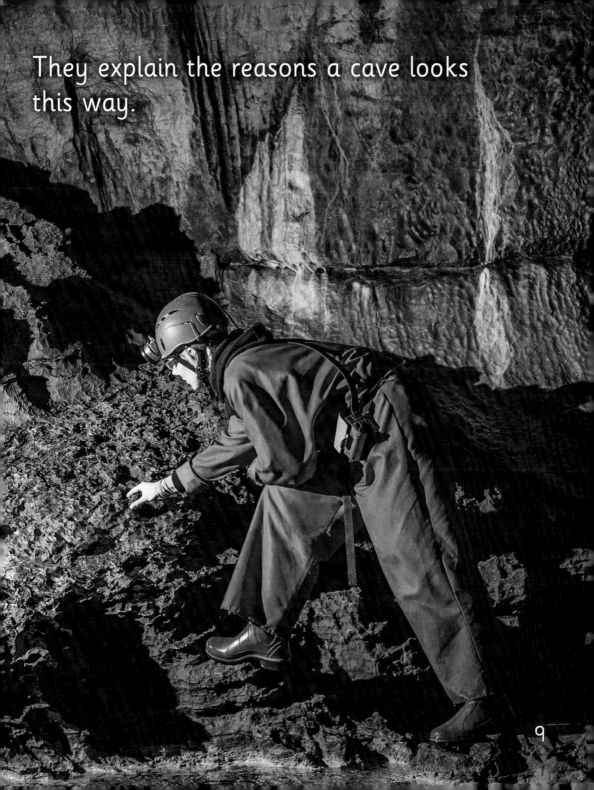

They explain the reasons a cave looks this way.

There are lots of ways of exploring caves.

diving in a sea cave

clambering up rock

a team travelling down a stream

11

This is the biggest cave
people can visit.

Its name is Hang Son Doong.
There is a real forest in it!

These steps lead to the longest chain of caves you can visit.

14

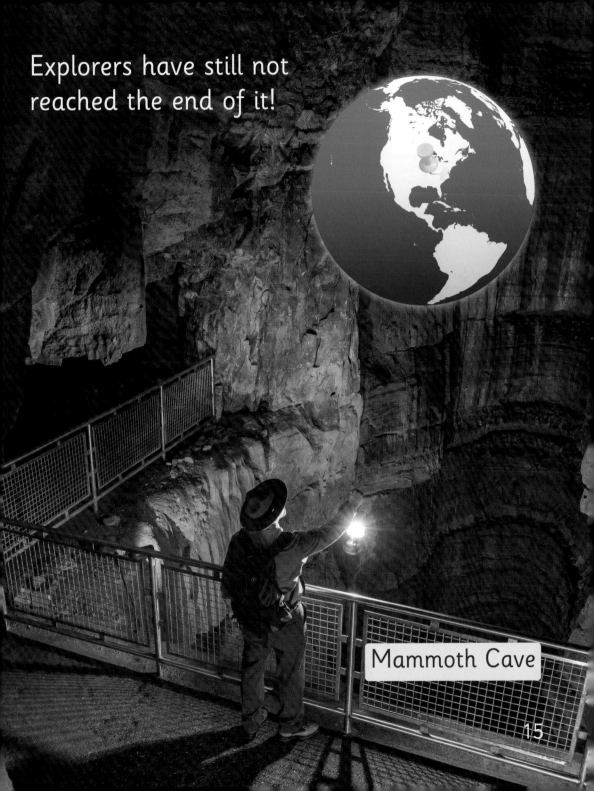

Explorers have still not reached the end of it!

Mammoth Cave

This cave looks like a dream, but it is real!

It was formed by waves in a big lake.

17

Caves made by people

Do you dream of living in a cave?

People have been living here for at least 3000 years.

Cave kit

There are lots of caves that families can visit!

This is what you may need.

torch

helmet

coat

boots

 Review: After reading

Use your assessment from hearing the children read to choose any GPCs, words or tricky words that need additional practice.

Read 1: Decoding

- Focus on spellings of /ai/ and /ee/ sounds.
- Look together at pages 4 and 5. Ask the children to find words with the /ai/ sound. (*cave, waves*) Turn to page 6. Can the children find the /ai/ sound but spelt differently? (*ai – rain*)
- Look together at pages 8 and 9. Ask the children to find two words that contain the /ee/ sound. (*stories, reasons*) Ask them to point to the letters that make this sound in each word. (*ie, ea*)

Read 2: Prosody

- Model reading each page with expression to the children. After you have read each page, ask the children to have a go at reading with expression.
- Show the children how you pause at commas to make longer sentences easier to understand.

Read 3: Comprehension

- Turn to pages 22 and 23 and use the pictures to talk about the different caves explored in this book. Which is the children's favourite cave?
- For every question ask the children how they know the answer. Ask:
  - On pages 4 to 5 and 6 in what ways are caves formed? (*sea against the cliffs, leaking rain*)
  - On page 8, what sort of stories might a cave tell? (e.g. *how it was formed and why it looks the way it does*)
  - What is the name of the biggest cave you can visit? (*Hang Son Doong*) Explain that the map shows that this cave is in Vietnam.
  - What is the name of the longest chain of caves you can visit? (*Mammoth Cave*) The map shows that this cave is in the USA.
  - How were the caves on pages 16 and 17 made? (*by waves in a lake*) Explain that these caves are in Chile, and they are called the Marble Caves.
  - What features does this book have which are often found in non-fiction books? (e.g. *contents list, photos, labels, globes/maps*)